S**

OTHER

EXPLORATIONS

Finding the Female in Divinity

"I am the invisible in the visible,
unnamed but always present.
I am the energy in the dance of the helix,
the spark that speaks to spark...
I am the life force that activates the egg,
that sends the sap
through the veins of the shamrock.
I am the dynamic of the sun,
giving all life...
I am the momentum
in the intensity of your coupling.
Wherever there is energy, vitality,
power and movement,
light and love,
there—there, I AM."
        Sophia, "Four in Three in One"

POEMS BY PAT PARNELL

Peter E. Randall Publisher
Portsmouth, New Hampshire
2001

Acknowledgments

Grateful acknowledgment is made to the following, in which some of these poems appeared in earlier versions: *Compass Rose, the White Pines College Journal of the Literary and Visual Arts; Currents II;* Exeter, N.H., *News Letter; HER WORDS, Poems for the Great Goddess; High on Poetry* CD; *The Journal; The New Hampshire College Journal;* The Poetry Vending Machine; *Poets' Touchstone; Re-Imagining; Return of the Goddess 1999; Under the Legislature of Stars,* 62 New Hampshire Poets; *Voices from the Center; Garden Lane;* and *Wordplay.*

Peter E. Randall Publisher
Box 4726, Portsmouth, NH 03802

Distributed by
        University Press of New England
        Hanover and London

        Library of Congress Cataloging-in-Publication Data
Parnell, Pat
    Snake woman and other explorations : finding the female in divinity
/poems by Pat Parnell.
        p. cm.
    ISBN 0-914339-94-X
    1. Goddess religion--Poetry. 2. Women and religion--Poetry.
    3. Goddesses--Poetry. 4. Religious poetry, American. I. Title.

PS3616.A76 S63 2001
811'.54--dc21

                                                                2001031932

For Dolores Kendrick
mentor and friend,
who helped me find my voice,
and for Burleigh Mutén
who first inspired me to reimagine
Medusa

Many thanks to my writing groups,
whose comments and support
are key elements of my writing process;
to Hildred Crill and Kimberly Cloutier-Green
for their careful, thorough, critical readings;
and a special thank-you to Muriel Stubbs with her acute
sensitivity to the right word in the right place.

For their invaluable assistance special thank-yous to Doug
Cellineri, chair of design and media arts at White Pines College,
for his digital magic with the cover photo
and to Peter Randall and Deidre Randall, for their patience,
support, and expertise.

With love, always, for my husband and family.

For Heather —
who helped make
today a fun
event — Pat
11/18/01

Contents

Art

Cover photograph, *Humanity and Sin*, photograph by Jessica E. Kern
Dancing Alpha and Omega, letters by Charlene Yelle   29
Venus of Kostionki, ink wash by Kate Parnell   34
Chartres Labyrinth, drawing by Robert Ferré   71
   (The St. Louis Labyrinth Project, www.labyrinthproject.com)
Seven-Circuit Labyrinth, courtesy of Loretta Rogers   72
   (www.angelfire.com/tn/SacredLabyrinth)
Black Flower, painting by Brigitte Keller   74

Notes

The quotation on p. 47 is from *Boethius, The Consolation of Philosophy*, translated with an Introduction and Notes by Richard Green. Copyright 1962. Bobbs-Merrill/Library of Liberal Arts, Indianapolis, Ind.

The citation from St. Augustine and the quotations on pages 49 and 53 are from *She Who Is* by Elizabeth A. Johnson. Copyright 1992 by Elizabeth A. Johnson. Crossroad Publishing Co, New York, N. Y.

The quotations on p. 50 and p. 55 are from *Sister of Wisdom, St.Hildegard's Theology of the Feminine* by Barbara Newman. Copyright 1987 by the Regents of the University of California. University of California Press, Berkeley and Los Angeles, California.

Introduction

"Theology is not logic, but poetry. Not syllogism, but story."

Since the summer of 1994, Sophia, Lady Wisdom, has been my guide in my quest for female manifestations of divinity. As a lector for my church, I was reviewing the readings for the Twentieth Sunday in Ordinary Time when I first encountered her in the Book of Proverbs, acting like any other hostess preparing for a dinner party: "Wisdom has dressed her meat, mixed her wine, yes, she has spread her table." Holy Wisdom, an attribute of God, the lector notes explained, is personified as a woman in Hebrew and Christian scripture.

Raised in strict Presbyterian male dominance and accustomed to the routine patriarchal style of the Catholic Church, I was amazed to discover Lady Wisdom and dismayed to realize that she had been hidden from me all my life. Eagerly I sought her, first in the Wisdom texts of the Hebrew scriptures and then in as many related works as I could find, especially those by feminist theologians.

What a rich banquet Wisdom has spread for me and for all who seek her!

Earlier that summer, I had encountered another manifestation of the Divine Feminine, the Kostionki "Venus" in the Hermitage Museum of St. Petersburg. I included her in my Russia travel article and thought I was finished with her, but she wasn't finished with me. The reading I was doing, and my resulting mental and spiritual ferment, led to the first poem in which I explored the female image of the divine, "Goddess: a Triptych."

That Christmas I did a book review of Burleigh Mutén's *Return of the Great Goddess*, the beginning of my warm friendship with Burleigh. During one of our brunch get-togethers, Burleigh told me of a ritual for Medusa in which she had participated. I said something polite, but I was really repelled—that horrible monster! Then I had another thought: "I know the patriarchal version of her legend. What might be the story from a feminist point of view?" Reimagining the narrative, I had a wonderful time devising a way for her to escape from Perseus and then creating adventures for a liberated snake goddess.

My "reimagining" approach has been influenced by my reading of the Re-Imagining Community. Their way of reexamining traditional approaches to religion in order to create a more inclusive theology and worship has been inspirational. I am pleased that some of my work, including the "O Tannenbaum" poem, has been published in the *Re-Imagining* journal.

To try re-imagining on your own, take an objective look at the familiar lawn figure of the Virgin Mary, standing on a blue planet Earth, sheltered by a scallop shell. Your eyes show you one interpretation of Mary; traditional theology tells the opposite story. Mary's body language, you can see, is serene, gracious, peaceful—no aggression or violence. The snake at her feet is not attacking her, not fighting against being crushed. His mouth is open in attack mode, but he is facing outward, warning away any threat to Mary. The Virgin and the snake are enemies, the theologians tell us, but the image-makers have tapped into a much older tradition: the Divine Feminine and her guardian serpent. And nobody notices!

(If you catch a suggestion of another Mary in the "Apotheosis" poem, a beloved guardian spirit—congratulations! You have a strong sense of literary allusion.)

As the book's title suggests, my poems are "explorations," examinations of the idea of the female in divinity as manifested in different individuals and different narratives. When I start exploring, I don't know where I will end up. I am frequently as surprised as the reader by my discoveries.

Some readers may be shocked, repelled, even horrified by some of the poems. (One writing group facilitator referred to the "Judith" poem as "Blasphemy!") Our own sons have told me, only half-joking, "We don't want our kids reading Grandma's poetry!"

My job as a poet is to search the expected for the unexpected and to proclaim what I have found. I hope that most readers will find their thinking and their spirituality stimulated by these approaches to what they may have been accepting without examination. Sara Maitland in her *A Big-Enough God, A Feminist's Search for a Joyful Theology*, writes, "We need a deeply imaginative meditation on the narratives and symbols of our past if we wish to co-create the future." Poets, she says, must be "embraced—and allowed, encouraged, loved, into running all the risks they want."

THE CHRONICLES
OF
SNAKE WOMAN

…...an interpretation suggests itself easily in
the case of the horrifying decapitated head of
Medusa. To decapitate=to castrate. The terror of
Medusa is thus a terror of castration....The hair
upon Medusa's head is frequently represented in
works of art in the form of snakes, and these once
again are derived from the castration complex....
The sight of Medusa's head makes the spectator
stiff with terror, turns him to stone.
>   SIGMUND FREUD, "Medusa's Head"
>   *Sexuality and the Psychology of Love*

Can we once again understand and appreciate
Female powers (and ourselves) in a state of
wholeness? Can we once again, with full respect,
look upon this most ancient, stirring, wild, laughing,
unpredictable, and supremely attractive face?
>   JANE CAPUTI, *Gossips, Gorgons, & Crones*

Snake Woman

I. Perseus and Medusa: A Retelling

Questing to behead the snake-haired monster,
Perseus, the shining one,
flies high above the foaming waves
on silver-winged sandals
to Medusa's rock beyond the edge of day.
Halcyone's seabirds have warned her, finding her
seated on the grass in her golden robe,
playing her flute.
His cap of darkness hides him,
but the birds know his coming
from the perturbation of the air.

Sighing, she rises to put on her curse again,
the masked crown, its brazen serpents
writhing and hissing. From the sacred vessels
she takes handfuls of menstrual blood
preserved for ritual. Great clots
dabble the visage, dripping from
brass forehead, mouth, pig ears,
bulging cheeks.

His invisibility ends. Oh, he is handsome
in his gleaming nakedness. Is this the hero
who will set her free?
Or will he end, like all the others,
a broken statue on the beach beyond?

The great curved shield, Athena's aegis, blazes.
Perseus sees in its shining surface
the Gorgon eyes goggle, the massive tongue
protrude between curving fangs.
Now the reflection ripples and changes.
It is his mother, Danaë, black hair
wild around her face
as though she had just awakened.

Now it is Medusa again, mirrored, staring
through bloodied eye sockets.

His manhood stiffens in bloodlust,
defying the horror.
With a great wordless cry,
Perseus, still shielding his vision,
swings his powerful sword
in the strength of his passion,
blinded to her recoil.

Clanging in climax, sword strikes mask,
knocking the bronze image from her shoulders,
and the reflected face rolls ringing to his feet.
Unmasked, Medusa, clutching her flute,
arcs from the sheer cliff
to the waiting sea.

Perseus, limp with victory, sees the splash
and smiles.
Still hiding his eyes, he
stabs the mask through an eye socket,
lifts it bleeding on his sword,
drops it, crown, serpents and all,
into a great bag, then draws tight the cords.
He wipes his weapon clean
on the grass. The silver-winged sandals
bear him triumphant to Athena.

Below, Medusa rises from the foam,
buoyed by golden sea serpents.
She grabs a horn of the leader
and climbs astride its neck. Laughing,
her long wine-dark hair swirling around her,
she plays a song of rejoicing.
Her comrades sing in high, clear voices,
swimming with her to the distant shore.

Athena, impervious to horror,
fuses trophy to shield

to petrify her enemies. Smiling,
she pokes her thumbs into the empty eye sockets.
She is snake goddess and owl goddess.
She can keep secrets....
Medusa is free.

II. Interview with a Snake Goddess

Perhaps our coupling was inevitable.
Is it rape if it is fate?
You might call it mutual rape,
each of us pursuing our passion
on the other.

I always knew where he was,
dreamed, despite myself, of his beauty
on my island.

Someone told him I had survived,
and then he came hunting me,
angry at the sham of his heroic deed.
But he did do
what a hero does—overcome the monster,
save the beautiful maiden—even if
not quite the way he thought.

Our single coupling gave him immortality,
but could not stop his aging.
Finally, his father Zeus took pity
on him, found a magic spell to
halt the years, saving him from the fate
of Tithonus, grasshopper man.
But the spell could not turn back
the clock. He's perpetually sixty-two. Heroes
do not age well.

I? I am whatever age I choose. Thirty-five
this week, I think. I am never alone.
My comrades braid themselves around my head,

coil close beside me when I sleep.
I am their sun-warmed rock, their cave
of hibernation. They nest in the secret places
of my body.

A snake goddess is anachronistic now.
Once our serpents were holy,
symbols of death and rebirth, immortality,
cherished in temples around the world.

Now I am Snake Woman.
The police come for me
when snakes escape. I charm them
out of heating vents and plumbing systems.
Talk to them, ask them if they want to return
to the owner who thought it would be fun
to have a giant python as a pet.
Some prefer the zoo, or their rain forest, and I
take them there. Some stay with me, and some
I leave in basement storage areas, where they
thrive on mice and beetles. "Just bang on the door
before you enter," I warn.
"The snake will get out of your way."

Sometimes I visit snake handlers in their churches,
honoring this echo of ancient days.
I talk with rattlesnakes and copperheads,
calm them, lay my hands on the bitten
to heal them.
Today, when nature exists
only to be used,
I am an entertainer,
charming snakes at the circus.
I play my flute, and, half upright,
they sway to the music. They wind themselves
around my upheld arms and couple in a caduceus
at my waist. Perseus is frightened of them,
hates them, but still he cannot leave me.
He is the sword swallower
in the next tent, swallowing the sword he used

to claim my mask. There aren't many jobs
for elderly heroes.

He was a king for a while, but old kings
do not last against the next generation
of strong young glory seekers.
When the invasion came,
we rescued him, my snakes and I.

For a while, we traveled with the gypsies.
They understood.

We are still linked, together through millennia.
Not by lust—gone with that one coupling—but
linked by our angers, long quiescent, by
our memories, by habit and inertia, mutual
accommodation, a sort of caring,

I can't foresee the future, but I sense a change
coming. One of my serpents twists himself
into a Möbius strip,
a one-edged single surface, biting his tail.
Where on this endless surface am I?
And where am I going?

III. Lilith

> "You can have me if you can catch me." She came
> to me like an angel from heaven. . . . This beautiful
> naked girl's body, pretty blond diamond shapes all
> over her. A rattlesnake head, and her tongue was
> just like a rattlesnake's too, sticking out at me.
> Jesco White, "The Dancing Outlaw"
> (WNPB-Morgantown, West Virginia)

Lilith is our daughter,
child of our one-time coupling, hero
and snake goddess joining in frenzy.

Our passion and anger
are mixed in her. She was a handful,
growing up. Wild, mischievous, changeable—
neither her father nor I could manage her.
She follows no law but her own.

She was Adam's first wife.
Motherlike, I warned her it wouldn't work.
I knew Yahweh,
him and his pretty little garden
and all his rules and regulations.

But she wanted the new-formed man,
innocent, unaware, someone she
could shape, make her mate.
But even new-formed, he was still
a man. Wanted his woman subservient.

She is her father's daughter, proud,
hot-headed, subservient to no one.
She escaped to the Red Sea, her
red hair a comet's tail behind her. Yahweh
sent his angels after her, but she was bold.
She pronounced the unpronounceable name,
and the angels fled in terror.

Some say she was the serpent that tempted Eve,
making trouble for the second wife.
In the Sistine Chapel, Michelangelo
painted the serpent with breasts
and a woman's face and hair.
I asked her one day, and she laughed.

But after Eden she came to Eve
when Adam was in the fields. Showed her—the
poor innocent—the wifely arts. Cooking, sewing,
spinning and weaving, preserving food.
Birthing, nurturing.
"Someone had to help her out," she told me.
Not the arts of the bed, though. "She won't
need them with him," she said and laughed.

She visited Solomon as Queen of Sheba,
testing him with her wisdom, teasing him with riddles.
He sang of his love for her, the Dark Goddess,
in the Song of Songs, and she bore his son.
I was a grandmother, tying a red thread
on the baby's cradle.

The story-tellers called her Demon
for daring to challenge the king.
They loaded all their fears on her, the scapegoat.
Beware of Lilith, the story tellers say.
She hides behind your mirrors, watching you.
All mirrors, they say, are Lilith's gateway
to her caves beneath the sea.

Throughout the years she has been
viewed with dread—and fascination.
Eternal Temptress, incubus and succubus,
Satan's Bride, mother of demons,
Kayn aynhoreh, the Evil Eye.
She was blamed for witches, those poor women.
And she and I were helpless, watching, able only
to ease their suffering as they burned to death.

I am proud to be her mother.
We are her parents, but she transcends us,
the Uroboric serpent,
joining humanity and divinity.
Queen of the South,
she will arise in Judgment on the Last Day.

She combines the wisdom of the body,
the wisdom of the mind, the wisdom
of the spirit, a sacred trinity. Through dreams
she teaches the joy of complete union, the
promise Adam wouldn't give her.

But woe to those who violate her vision,
demean love, deny it, take it by force.
She leaves them with perpetual priapism,

Adam-like, always unsatisfied,
while she returns, laughing,
triumphant, to her castle on the Red Sea,
leaving her star-shaped footprints on the shore.

IV. Snake Woman at the Circus

In the tent next to the sword swallower,
Snake Woman swallows serpents.

She holds the snake behind the head.
Its body curls briefly around her wrist,
then hangs straight.
Snake Woman throws back her head,
opening her mouth
all the way to her anus.

The snake is stiff as a sword.
It slips down slowly and easily, tail first.
Snake woman raises her arms in triumph.
Her breasts, nipples erect,
bulge against her thin blouse.
Drums roll.

She smiles at the crowd, mouth
open wide. The snake sticks out its head,
yellow eyes surveying the crowd,
forked tongue flicking.

At this point, there is always
a man who faints. Two small
children who vomit into
their pink cotton candy.

The sword swallower dares not swallow.
He would split his esophagus on the
sword edge. But Snake Woman swallows.
Her throat caresses the smooth scales.
The snake ripples in response.
More drums roll. Snake Woman

draws out the snake, extended full length.
She grabs the tail with her other hand
and holds the snake aloft, stretched out,
bluegreen scales glittering.

Then she wraps the snake around
her waist, like rolls of fat,
and ducks behind the tent
for a quick smoke.

V. Snake Woman Meets Modern Medicine

Snake Woman carries in her womb
the mother serpent nesting, circled
around a clutch of eggs, ten eggs.

Snake Woman
nourishes the serpent from her body.
The eggs are warm
in the amniotic fluid.

Here is Snake Woman,
stiff and angry, in the white sheets
of a hospital bed,
not squatting on the dirt floor
of the birthing cave.

It is time. The eggs split.
Bright yellow eyes peer
into the darkness.
The fetal monitor implodes,
trying to count the heartbeats.
The mother serpent
bites through the placenta.
She squirms through the dilated cervix
in a rush of blood.

White and sterile, rubber gloved,
the doctor's hands
thrust into Snake Woman,

spreading wide the vagina.
Nature is not enough.

When he jerks backward,
the mother serpent has grabbed his wrist,
biting through the latex,
and baby snakes hang from each finger,
wriggling.

VI. Medusa and Hecate

Where three roads meet, she waits for me
at the dark of the moon.
I have summoned her, Hecate,
underworld goddess, queen of witches
and hidden knowledge.
Her hands hold up three torches,
lighting each roadway.
Her three faces, lit by torch flare, gaze
down each distant prospect.

Cerberus, her three-headed dog,
crouches at her ankles.
He sniffs my feet, gives me a rough paw
to shake. Her snake and mine touch noses briefly,
flick tongues in greeting.

Others fear her, but I know Hecate:
she is midwife also, goddess of childbirth,
of beginnings.
She was there for my first breath,
there for our daughter's star-crossed birth.
Can she help me as I strain,
heavy with uncertainty?

Her thin fingers, dry as lizard skin,
grip my chin, tilt my head, turn it.
Her torch lights my face,
almost close enough to sear my cheek.

All I can see is gold. I do not flinch.
Her eyes pierce my mind,
stare beyond it.

"You have three choices, child.
You can continue
as you are. This right-hand road
will carry you the way you have been traveling,
the circus of your life.

"Or you can turn here and come with me
to the realm of the old deities, the choice
you once refused.
Gods and Goddesses who wait out millennia,
hoping for revival. Spending their days
flirting, gossiping, telling lies, bragging
of their exploits and their powers.
Believing their reign will come around again."

"And the third choice?"

"Go forward the way you came. Not to your island.
Time has moved on, in its spiral cycle.
The old Greeks knew:
you can't walk the same road twice.
But you can begin again,
find your new future."

"Will I still be Snake Woman?"

"Try it and see."

VII. Apotheosis of Medusa

Flaming with anger and despair, Perseus is hunting
        Medusa. His newly sharpened sword gleaming,
        he runs shouting through the city streets. "Where
        are you, you snake charmer! I will destroy you, as
        you have destroyed me!" He has been drinking.

In the park in front of the cathedral, Medusa, young and
        beautiful again, sits cross-legged on a great rock
        playing her flute, her golden robe wrapped round
        her. Three of her snakes have braided themselves
        into a crown for her wine-dark hair. Two, with green
        and purple scales shining, interlace in a caduceus
        on an oak sapling before her, their coupling timed to
        the rhythm of her music. Her other snakes circle
        around the pair, swaying half-erect to her song.

Suddenly Perseus is there, enraged. "You have ruined my
        life, you and your youth and beauty." The circus has
        dismissed him, telling him he is too old for Medusa.
        Him, the greatest sword swallower of all time—
        replaced with a smouldering young fire-eater! He is sobbing.
        "What can I do? Where can I go?" Eternity confronts
        him, empty, aimless. "You and your slimy snakes."
        He has always hated them. "But I'll get even.
        Now I'll finish what I started so long ago."

Medusa rises, her serpent crown uncoiling. Protecting her,
        the snakes are a hissing army, heads back, fangs
        bared. Perseus, sword flashing, attacks in frenzy.
        Blinded by bloodlust he does not see Medusa
        fade into invisibility against the shrubbery.

With the serpents shredded at his feet, Perseus turns his
        bloody sword toward Medusa. Where is she?
        "Snake Woman!" With a great cry, Perseus rushes
        in search of her, hacking the underbrush.

Quickly Medusa gathers her bloodied companions into her
        robe. Where to hide? The open doors of the cathedral—
        beckon like the doorway of the cave on her island rock
        beyond the edge of day.

Inside, she hears a soft call, "Come to me, Snake Woman."
        Halfway down one side of the vast darkness, a low
        light beckons, the sanctuary of Mary, Queen of

Heaven. Her great statue wears a blue robe and a
crown of stars. Her serpent is beneath her heel.
Candles flicker around her. The statue glows a welcome
from within. "Cast your friends before me," Mary says.
"I will heal them." Rejoined, the snakes curl at
the statue's feet, and Medusa's robe gleams golden,
cleansed.

"Snake Woman, are you here?" Perseus's great cry fills
the cathedral. "Come," says Mary, holding out her
hand. "I am Queen of Snake Goddesses. I will
hide you." She draws Medusa into herself as
Perseus, sword ready, rushes past.

Medusa has found a home. The statue is hollow, airy, much
larger on the inside than on the outside. The smooth
plaster walls work like one-way glass: all that
happens in the cathedral is a panorama for Medusa.
She sleeps coiled in the statue's base. There is
even room for her to play her flute. Her snakes are
happy to stay curled with the painted one at Mary's heel.

Sometimes at night Mary and Medusa fly together hand
in hand through the heavens, visiting Mary's
realm. The sky is full of snakes. Ophiuchus,
Serpent-Bearer, with his writhing Serpens, greets
them, Asclepius, who learned from serpents how to
revive the dead. The fire-breathing Draco, swishing
his double tail, rears to hug Medusa as they fly by,
seeking Perseus' constellation in the northern sky.
The Eye of the Medusa mask winks at them as they
buzz around the starry hero, teasing, like a pair of
mosquitoes. Perseid meteors shower them with stardust
as they head home.

Perseus, earthbound, lives in the homeless shelter in the
cathedral basement, peeling potatoes and washing
dishes for his keep. His sword chops sausages for
the cabbage soup. He spends his mornings searching
the park for Medusa, his afternoons in prayer

before the statue of the Virgin. He does not see all
the snake eyes staring at him below the blue robe.
Medusa is near, somewhere, he is sure, he feels her
presence, but always she eludes him. Sometimes he
thinks he hears flute music, but he pushes that
fantasy firmly away.

One day a cleaning woman, in great agitation, reports a
miracle to the cathedral administrator. "There are
extra snakes at the feet of Blessed Mother. Her
statue glows from within. And I heard music playing."
The cleric doesn't bother to check. "Too much *vino*,"
he decides, and transfers her to scrubbing toilets.
The other cleaning women say nothing. They know
what they know. And when they have carefully dusted
the snakes—and the starry crown—they kneel before the
Queen of Heaven a few extra moments in silent prayer.

CELEBRATING SHEILA-NA-GIG

Sheila-na-gig is the Celtic divinity, found in
France, England, Scotland, and Ireland, over
church doorways, on bridges and towers and
castle walls, who protects against enemies
with the power of female sexuality. She is
often portrayed squatting frog-like in the
birthing position, spreading her genitals with
her fingers to show the source of her power.
Rabelais tells the story of the woman who frightened
away the Devil by showing him her vulva. That's
Sheila-na-gig.

Hunkered in her niche in the window wall,
Sheila-na-gig glares into the hall of the great keep,
reminding entertainers in medieval gowns:
"Underneath your velvet, your lace and fake pearls,
underneath your makeup and your soft young flesh,
your singing and dancing,
I am what endures, the sinew, the bone, the strength."
                    from *An Irish Journal*, 1993, Bunratty Castle
                                    Pat Parnell

Snake Woman

For the Ballylarkin Sheila

Sheila-na-gig, you dance all over Ireland
among the fuchsia and montbrettia,
your gray or brown or black
decked with their purple, red, and orange,
celebrating life.

We have forgotten your origins,
Sheila-na-gig,
the Celtic homesteads whose portals you guarded.
Now you embarrass us.
We make guesses about you: fertility goddess,
protector against the evil eye,
a warning against the horrors
of female sexuality.

But the old Celts knew both male and female
in the strength of the sexual force.
Their warriors rushed into battle
aroused by blood lust,
their giant erections matching their giant swords,
bragging of the power of their virility.

They put your crouching figure
over their doorways,
posed in the birthing squat, horseshoe shaped,
to proclaim the power of woman,
protector of the home.

As guardian, you wear your death's head aspect,
grinning.
Withered breasts hang from your skeletal ribs.
Your fingers spread wide your lips
in their dreadful vertical grin,
warning strangers, "I am woman. I am power.
Don't menace me or mine."

Later years have denied you,
Sheila-na-gig.
The monks passing beneath you
averted their eyes, afraid
lest you haunt their dreams.

Buried in graveyards,
you refused to die.
You were thrown into rivers,
a baptism that couldn't wash away your strength.

We find you still, worn by time, on old bridges,
round towers, standing stones,
the entrances of castles and churches.
To museums you are dusty unimportant artifact.
We label you superstition, averting our eyes
like the medieval monks.
To us you are vulgar, obscene,
but you escape our censure.
Crouching, leaping, dancing, grinning,
you are unstoppable,
life force unveiled, unashamed.

I hang your image by my bedside, Ballylarkin Sheila.
Guard my household. I ask your strength
for me and mine.

 Alpha
and
Omega

Meditation, St. Mark's Church, Stratford, Connecticut

Jesus is the Alpha male, Sheila-na-gig is Omega, the end
that leads to the beginning, the good-luck horseshoe,
the tomb and the womb.

At the processional hymn
the golden symbols,
Alpha and Omega,
Jesus and Sheila,
jump from their carvings, from
the gray marble slab
fronting the green marble altar.

At the foot of the sanctuary steps
they are clogging, good old
mountain breakdown,
the letters' curve their pelvis,
the serifs their dancing feet.

Now both up on one toe
pirouetting. He twirls her en pointe, her
other leg extended. Next he crouches
into a Russian dance, heels clicking,
legs flying quickly, while Sheila stands,
immobile, one-legged like a stork,
instep against knee.

Sheila likes the Irish stepdance,
riverdance,
where only feet and legs move
in intense synchronicity.

Now they are tapdancing, back and forth
before the altar, faster, faster,

the flames from the altar candles
glinting on their gold.

Like old-time vaudeville stars, they hoof it
up the proscenium, one on each side,
tapping up and dropping back,
higher and higher each time,
then jumping gracefully down.

Acrobats,
curving their long legs around the candelabras,
they swing back and forth
above the Creed. Sheila throws herself
in a triple somersault, Alpha catching,
ankles hooked around ankles.
They swing and swing again, and he
tosses her to catch the shining trapeze
at the height of her golden arc.

At the Consecration, they drop
to kneel at the altar, then with the bells
that only they can hear, they cartwheel
down the aisle,
St. Catherine's Wheel, Wheel of the Sun.

Lord and Lady of the Dance,
they do a soft shoe on top of the organ,
keeping time to the Communion hymn,
the slight scuffing of their feet
the air breathing in the pipes.

Suddenly shrinking, they skate like water bugs
on the surface of the holy water font,
leaping to sprinkle one another in blessing.

Ite, Missa est, and, their own size again,
they flip to the beat of the recessional hymn
across the backs of the emptying pews.
Alone they nestle themselves
into their carved niches,
to pulse and glow until the music
begins again.

Síle-na-gCíoch

Let's join the maiden voyage
of the ferryboat christened *Sheila-na-Gig*.
She will open herself wide
to receive us in our automobiles, two by two.

Sheila-na-Gig will carry us
beyond the Ninth Wave,
beyond Tír-na-n´Og, land
of perpetual youth.

On her wide sunlit upper deck,
we ladle soup from her bronze cauldron,
dine on the roasted venison
hunters bring in gratitude for their luck,
eat the first fruits of the harvest,
dedicated to Sheila.

We drink her sacred mead,
sing her sacred songs,
dance her sacred dances.

When we weary, we nestle
in a warm nook,
as if lulled in a great water bed.
In our sleep, Sheila cleanses our minds
until they are as placid as an unborn child's.
The images of our dreams
rise at her bidding
from our ancient souls.

And when we wake,
Sheila-na-Gig will ferry us home,
opening herself wide as we drive off
in our shining, refurbished cars.
Returned, we take up our lives again
with the new strength
that is her gift to us.
Sláinte, Sheila!

Sheila at the Museum

Kildare St., Dublin

Seven Sheilas sit on the shelves
in the cellar of the National Museum.
Eyes that saw far
over valley and forest
now gaze through the darkness
down the long paths of memory:
enemies frightened away,
battles won,
the Evil Eye averted;
good luck to friends;
babies that came safely
after prayer and sacred touching.

Here the Sheilas find sanctuary
as in cave or crypt or catacomb.
Here they are safe
from vandalism of weather,
vandalism of those
who call them
witch, idol, sacrilege,
Irish pornography.

They are as rough and ashen
as peat fires banked for the night.
Protected at their heart
are the glowing coals of their strength.
Cherish them, curator.
They are still Erin's
guardian spirits.

Sheila the Hat

(for the Rahara Sheila, County Roscommon)

Sheila-na-gig, I will make myself a hat
in your image. The fabric is grey and rough,
like the keystone in which you are carved
over the old church doorway.
Your hands hold open your lips
so they fit snugly over my ears.
My head is a giant egg you are laying
or the last bit of a breech birth
you are pushing out of yourself.

I will wear you skiing
when the bright winter sun shines blinding
off the snow.
Your lips clutch tight,
warming me with your body heat.
You crouch above my forehead, facing
into the wind, shading my eyes.
Your hands clasp under my chin,
your legs cross over my chest,
hugging close.
Your thick braids swing across my shoulders,
thumping,
as we tuck, twist, and turn, speeding
down the slope.

The wind of our race
flattens your breasts against your rib cage.
Your Gaelic battle cry cheers me on.
Everyone who sees you will say,
"What a great hat!"

Venus of Kostionki   ink wash by Kate Parnell

REDISCOVERING
THE GODDESS

In *The Masks of God: Primitive Mythology*, Joseph Campbell describes the finding in Kostyenki, (as he spells it) by the river Don of the female figures he calls Our Lady of the Mammoths. He dates them to the Paleolithic, calling them the "first objects of worship of the species Homo Sapiens."

Vicki Noble, in her *Shakti Woman*, cites recent British research which dates the earliest Great Goddess figures to up to three million years ago. "The earliest humans," she says, "created images of the divine woman from stone, the forms of which still, amazingly, survive."

Snake Woman

Goddess: A Triptych

*To the Kostionki 'Venus,' 23,000 B.C.E., the
Hermitage Museum, St. Petersburg, Russia*

Panel 1

My cupped hand could shelter you.

You stand as you have stood,
white stone,
for twenty-five thousand years.

Your head is bowed
toward your heavy hanging breasts.
A wide ceremonial necklace vees between them.
Your hands clasp loosely over your broad belly,
above the pyramid of your femaleness,
your swelling thighs.

Your head is a great angled ball,
hair etched tight in rows.
Your featureless face hides   mischief   demureness
that secret smile   wisdom   love
There is shyness in your bent head.
You are like a young girl
observing with wonder the richness
of your full new body.

Did the woman who carved you dip her thumbs
into ground limestone
and polish the great globes of your breasts,
or were they rubbed smooth by generations of women
willing their milk?
Were you kept secluded, only for woman's ritual,
or were you there for daily life, guardian of the hearth?
I
  know your sister, goddess,
your Willendorf twin.

Across thousands of miles and years, your image spread
and was cherished. Honored. Kept safe.
How many of your sisters lie hidden still
in caves, in tombs, in buried sanctuaries?
Now you are in a glass case, waiting.

Panel 2

What can we call you, lady?
Our language has no name for you, divine femina.
Even "goddess" is a patriarchal word.
Finding you, the excavators labeled you "Venus"
in jest, mocking your womanhood.

Our culture scorns you.
We venerate another Venus,
your neighbor in the next exhibit hall.
Aphrodite, androgynous sprite,
born of your sea foam,
she is your daughter, your young self,
the sliver of a crescent moon
to your full moon.

The sculptor who carved her, fantasizing:
the tall young slave boy, bending willow-like
to serve the wine
at last night's feast. The artist's hand creates
the face of a sexless woman, the body of a
just-pubescent girl. Long slim legs, slim hips,
flat belly. She denies her femaleness. One hand
covers her small breasts, the other the bare triangle.
This slim Eve, forever poised on the brink of life—
taught to worship her, we hate ourselves,
denying you, goddess,
deriding your body and ours.

In idolatry we torture ourselves,
striving for her perfection.
We pare the rind of our skin and pierce our flesh,
immolating ourselves, a sacrifice at her altar.

School girl, actress, singer, dancer, gymnast,
we ravage ourselves in her image.

Our worship fixates us—and her.
Nor she nor we can grow nor change.

Her head is turned away from us,
marble eyes staring beyond us
into infinity.
She does not see our pain.

Panel 3

I recognize you, goddess,
holy one from the age of the mammoth.
You are human: my mother, my sister.
The woman in the supermarket, at the mall,
on the beach. In my mirror.

Can we see your strength? Your beauty?
See youth and age as one, the movement of the current
from mountain spring to ocean depth.
You are fulfillment of all beginnings.
You have borne life,
carried your burdens, done your work.
Your body shows the weight of your role.
You bear your years with pride.
You have endured.
Your dignity is our affirmation.
You have the courage of acceptance;
nothing female is alien to you.

In the glass of your case, goddess,
I see myself and you.
Across the millennia you recognize me,
calling my name.
From your sanctuary you whisper,
"Hail, daughter, sister, self."

In one version of the Ariadne legend, she becomes the consort of the god Dionysus, instructing his female followers in the ritual dance. At her death, he makes her a goddess and places her crown in the heavens as a circle of stars.

Ariadne on Naxos
for S. M. K.

The ship is almost to the horizon. Only its black sails make it visible. Theseus is so full of pride at what he calls his great victory, he will not think to change them. I am not surprised that he deserted me. Not after last night.

Crete was too small for me. I wanted to know what lies beyond our circle of sea, discover where the ships come from that visit our island. "No," my father said, "You will live in Crete, in the life I have planned for you." Then Theseus came, and I knew he could take me away. He promised. I stole my father's sword for him and told him how to use the ball of yarn I gave him.

After the killing, we fled with the rescued Athenians. I exulted at my freedom. "They will have a festival for us in Athens," I proclaimed joyfully, "celebrating your strength and my wisdom. We have released the city from the sacrifice." He did not reply. Instead, he led me to a cave on this island where we had stopped to rest for the night. Our first chance to be alone together. On the dry sand within the cave, he laid his cloak, then tried to make me recline. "No," I told him, heady with our triumph. "You lie there and I will mount you, as I mount the bulls in the bull leaping." "That is not the Athenian way," he said, angry. "Greek women are submissive to their men." "Ha!" I was becoming angry too. "I am Ariadne of the lovely locks, a Princess and a Priestess. I lead the dance on my beautiful dancing floor. In the games, I am the fastest runner. In the bull leaping, I do more somersaults than any other, vaulting between the bull's horns and down his back. I would not submit to my father when he tried to keep me on Crete. I do not submit to anyone."

At that moment the Athenian maidens came to the cave, dancing to their pipes and timbrels. "Theseus," they called, "come and celebrate. You have killed the monster and set us free." He turned from me and left.

Suddenly, I did not feel like rejoicing. Hideous as he was, the monster was my half-brother. When he was a baby, I went into the labyrinth every day, guided by the thread Daedalus gave me. I cleaned him, gave him his bottle, tickled his shaggy tummy. But he grew so fast. One day he came at me. Only my speed in running and the guiding thread saved me. Chasing me, he took a wrong turn and lost himself in his own maze. I got away, and I never went back. But I grieved last night for the calf-baby I had cared for and loved. I fell asleep, and when I awoke, the cloak was gone and so was Theseus. He will celebrate his victory in isolated splendor, with no one claiming a share in the glory. And he will have his choice of Athenian maidens, all properly submissive.

So here I am, alone on this island. Free of my father, who would have kept me confined. Free of the hero who could not accept my strength. What next on this uncharted journey?

> *"Turn around; I have come to you in my*
> *dragon chariot. Turn around; I have*
> *brought you a crown of stars."*

A Holiday Celebration for the Goddess

O Tannenbaum

*Christmas trees: ritually murdered and
dismembered....subliminally symbolic of the
massacred and dismembered Goddess....cut
down, dragged indoors, dolled-up....*
MARY DALY, "Word-Web Three," *Wickedary*

When all the family is gone to bed, tree unplugged,
curtains drawn, lamps turned off,
doors closed to keep the room cool,
she connects the Christmas lights
to her own energy, stored from summer sun,
the voltage that keeps her needles green.

Then, shimmering in her jeweled ball gown,
she dances, swirling around the room
on the three feet of the tree stand, humming her carol.
"How lovely are my branches!"
Her Christmas bells jingle, ornaments sparkle,
as she juggles the candy canes—three at a time,
five, ten, twelve—all in the air,
a kaleidoscope of red and white.

The cat watches from her corner.

"How do these tree needles
get all over the carpet?" scolds Mother,
busy vacuuming the next morning.
Both tree and cat are silent.

After the holiday, dragged outdoors,
she fills a hollow in the woods,
a shelter for field mice and voles,
holding them safe in her outstretched arms,
hiding them from the scavenging cat.

Rain and snow recycle her
as bright green moss or white Mayflowers
or fiddle-headed ferns.

Don't grieve for the Goddess, Mary Daly;
like her tree, she flourishes, immortal:
glory of the solstice, solace of winter,
promise of spring.

Seeking the Feminine Principle in the Universe

SOPHIA, "THE BREATH OF THE POWER OF GOD"
(Wisdom 7:25)

The female divine has been hidden, almost destroyed, as Perseus tried to destroy Medusa, but if we look for her, she is still there, even in the Hebrew and Christian scriptures. There she can be found as Lady Wisdom, female aspect of Divinity. Sapientia. Sophia.

Sophia, God's Wisdom

Wisdom inspireth life into her children,
and protecteth them that seek after her...
and God loveth them that love her.
Ecclesiasticus 4, 12-15

Journal, Nov. 7—In the church basement classroom where we study Wisdom, she eludes us, laughing when we think to grasp her. In the corner near the stage, the wooden cut-out Christmas tree, star-topped, waits to be placed by the altar with all the Christmas wishes—the Giving Tree. The portable chalkboard stands in front of it to hide it, but the great green skirt of the tree shows wide and firm below. The tree rises in its corner, rising through the roof, rising to the heavens, a Nutcracker tree. The yellow-painted star peers over the top of the chalkboard, watching us. The star is Sophia, letting us glimpse her, guiding us as she guided the Wise Men, their Christmas Star, burning bright in the heavens at night, beckoning them to follow.

To Boethius, awaiting martyrdom,
she looked nine feet tall, piercing the ceiling of his cell,
sometimes rising to the heavens.
Her eyes burned "beyond the usual power of men."
Carrying her lily sceptre in one hand, books in the other,
she brought him the consolations of philosophy,
the strength to face his death.

Banished by fearful men,
she has hidden herself for centuries,
her Gnostic legends lost.
In Mary and the saints, we honor her attributes,
forgetting their origin. We see her in Scripture,
not as female but as metaphor.
In spite of all oppression,
she has been with us through the centuries, in disguise,
not deserting us, taking many forms,
waiting for us to be ready for her again.

She is the statue of Justice above the courthouse,
blindfolded, with her scales.
She is Columbia, promising a bright future
for America's ideals.

She is the Statue of Liberty, high in the harbor,
lifting her torch beside the golden door.

She is in strong women,
the wise, caring mother,
the teacher remembered best,
the friend and mentor, supportive,
pointing out possibilities, warning of hazards.
She is in queens and saints and union organizers,
Florence Nightingale, Jane Addams, Sojourner Truth.

> *Wisdom is publishing her message,*
> *crying it aloud in the open streets;*
> *never a gateway, but her voice is raised,*
> *echoing above the din of it.*
> Proverbs 1: 20-21

Eleanor Roosevelt visited our college once in the war years.
The diningroom echoed with sophomoric bravado.
"When she walks in, I'm not going to pay any attention."
"I'll just keep right on eating."
"Why should I stand for her?"
"She's just like anybody else."
No one used the word "charisma" then,
but when the door opened, the room filled
with her presence.
She walked quietly, nine feet tall in her dark red dress,
her eyes straight ahead,
as we all rose
in the transcendent silence.

Four in Three in One

"And so, the Father is Wisdom, and the Son is Wisdom, and the Holy Spirit is Wisdom, and together, not three Wisdoms, but one Wisdom."
                    ST. AUGUSTINE, *De Trinitate*

Sophia, Divine Wisdom,
you are in God, of God, distinct from God,
but we have not known you.
If the Trinity contains all of God,
in the Trinity, where are you?

Consider the miracle of the egg:
The fertile yolk, gold as the sun,
life-bearing as the sun.
The life-giving primordial sea in which it floats,
pellucid, protean, protein,
liquid atmosphere.
The shell, surrounding, protecting,
biosphere, solid womb.
I hold it end to end between my palms,
unable to crush it.
Are you in the egg, Sophia?

Can we see you, She Who Is,
in the triple helix,
spiraling symbol?
Infinite mix,
bending and intertwining
in its cosmic dance,
separation, recombination,
*"one source of life, new just order,
and quickening surprise."*

Patrick showed the Celts a shamrock,
three leaves, one plant,
each leaf a heart,
each separate, but an equal part of the whole.
Are you in the shamrock, Sophia?

Are you in the Celtic knot,
symbol of kingship,
like the shoulder brooch of Brian Boru?
Copper, pewter, bronze,
separate but interlocking,
the light striking off each strand,
a labyrinth the eye cannot resolve.

Hildegard of Bingen
saw the Trinity in the sun, "a single entity":
*"for the sun is bright, and its light blazes,
and in it burns the fire
that illuminates all the world."*
Do you burn in that sun, Sophia?

Freud envisioned a trinity of personality,
ego, superego, id,
separate but inseparable,
the rational, the ideal, the hidden drives
of darkness,
with the constant interplay of energies.
Are you hiding within me, Sophia?

Can we hear you in our music?
The Mozart *Divertimento*
teases us to follow.
Violin, viola, cello,
playing as one
in the vocalized singing of the strings.
Balanced, respectful, bowing to one another,
each creates a separate sound
that is one sound.

Our lives are filled with trinities, the mystic
in the commonplace, again and again ignored.
My sister's braids,
halfway down her back,
triple-plaited, gold glinting from
the brown.

Geometry's equilateral triangle,
the pyramids of the Egyptians and Mayans,
the pendentives in your dome, Sophia,
three the prime number,
all studied but not seen,
these metaphors of the divine.

Our most intimate moments are a trinity.
The he of it, the she of it, the it of it.
Our joining transcends our being.
We loose ourselves into a separate existence,
always there, always waiting for us
to reach it, to enter it, to slip lingering
away, dreaming of our return.
Where are you, Sophia, in all our unrecognized trinities,
the trinities that transcend our world, our knowing?

I am the invisible in the visible,
unnamed but always present.
I am the energy in the dance of the helix,
the spark that speaks to spark.
I am the golden glints of your sister's braids,
the gleam of the Celtic knot.
I am the life force that activates the egg,
that sends the sap
through the veins of the shamrock.
I am the dynamic of the sun,
giving all life.
I am the Euclidian perfection of the triangle,
the cosmic centering of the pyramid,
the four in three in one.
I am the force of your personality,
its animating strength.
I am the harmonies of divine music.
I am the momentum
in the intensity of your coupling.
Wherever there is energy, vitality,
power and movement,
light and love,
there—there, I AM.

RE-IMAGINING SCRIPTURAL TRADITION

...the word God refers to the sacred at the center of existence, the holy mystery that is all around us and within us....God is more than everything, and yet everything is in God.

MARCUS BORG, *Meeting Jesus Again for the First Time*

Human speech about God is analogical.... There is always more in the concept than the concept can bear.

ELIZABETH JOHNSON, *She Who Is*

Snake Woman

Meditation on the Visions
of Abbess Hildegard of Bingen
(1098-1179)

Just as she saw God draw Eve,
like a shining cloud,
from the side of His first son, Adam,
Eve, offspring and bride of Adam,
carrying within herself,
like a host of stars, all
the offspring of the human race,

so also she saw
God draw Ecclesia, Holy Church, from
the piercéd side of His son Jesus, crucified,
Ecclesia, offspring and bride of Christ,
carrying *all mirth and the joy of joys*
within her flaming heart,
the souls of all the blessed.

These birthing visions celebrate
the maternity of Adam, Jesus,
in the strength and beauty
of their femaleness.
Eve and Ecclesia glow glorious,
virid and seminal,
progenitors
and soul-bearers.

An Easter Song for Miriam

(Numbers 12: 1-16)

God has spit in my face.

The white flakes of my leprosy
fall to the ground
like the manna
He gives us for food.

I was just trying to help.

I, a woman, offered myself
as alternative for His Anointed One.
Therefore the anger of the Lord
is kindled against me.

Has the Lord spoken only through Moses?

Moses is my brother. I
saved his life, helping with the basket
that carried him on the river. It was my
cleverness
that suggested a wet nurse, his own mother,
to aid the daughter of the Pharaoh. I
stayed with him, bathed him,
changed him, fed him, loved him,
watched him grow. I

helped him escape
when he killed the Egyptian
who was beating a Jew.
And when he returned
to lead us to freedom, I
rallied the women to follow him. I
led the dance
through the parted waters as we sang my
song and celebrated our deliverance,
praising God's name.

Throughout this weary journey, my
well has followed us from camp to camp,
bursting from the earth
to solace us with water.

Now Moses is busy with his heathen bride.
He has no time for our people,
no time to listen to their woes. I
am a prophet, a healer, a counselor. I
have insight into troubled hearts.

But I
must not claim
to be my brother's equal.
That was too bold for God.

Banished from camp, I
sit here in exile,
shedding my pride
with my flaking skin.

Moses and Aaron
begged God's mercy for me.
And the people refuse
to continue the journey
until I
return. So much love
helps me bear my shame.

And I am grateful
He has not taken away my
gift of prophecy.
Down the millennia I
see another Messenger of God,
His own Son, born of a woman,
embracing women as his followers.

It is women who first find the empty tomb,
women who first hear that he is risen.

To Mary Magdalene, his favored disciple,
he first appears in Easter glory.
Mary the Mother,
Mary the disciple,
my sisters,
carrying my name.
They give me strength,
and all the holy women I
see following them. I
rejoice at my visions.

And when my banishment is over
and my flesh is clean again, I
will return to camp
singing the future, my
new song.

Rizpah

(2 Samuel 21: 9-15)

Now I watch
over my own bones only.
Our sons are buried, Saul,
and your grandsons, the bloodguilt
you bequeathed them expiated,
that poisoned the land,
and the rains have come again.

For six months I watched on this hillside,
guarding their impaled bodies,
driving off scavenger birds by day,
dogs and jackals at night,
keeping vigil over our dead.

When I dozed, their cries would wake me.
  "Mother, I'm cold."
  "Mother, I'm thirsty."
  "Mother, the foxes are eating my feet."
I—their mother, their grandmother—
I could not ease their pain.

The rain has soaked my robe,
worn threadbare these six months,
and the sackcloth blanket
where I sit on these rocks.
My hands lie in my lap, idle now,
my arms withered and black, the skin
tight to the bone, as their arms were.
My legs and feet are shriveled, mummy-like,
shrunken like theirs by the sun and wind.
My face must be as skull-like as theirs.
I saw the look the messenger gave me
when he came to tell me
of David's decree.

So, Saul, you and your sons and grandsons
lie together in the grave.
No festivities at the burial,
but after all the guilt and suffering,
it is an honorable end.

Only I am left, silent on this hillside,
waiting.
The great stakes stand empty now,
glistening black and bare in the life-giving rains.
Who will drive the dogs and birds from me?

Susanna

(Daniel 13: 1-63)

I see them look at me
when they think I'm not watching.
The two of them—our leaders, our judges,
musty-smelling old men
with dirt in their beards,
dirt caked in the creases of their necks.
Their dusty robes crack on the folds
from dry rot.
We women must bathe every month,
the law says, to purify ourselves.
They pour a little water over their fingers
before meals, their ritual washing.

They were chosen as Elders for their wisdom,
but they pervert that wisdom,
extorting bribes from the guilty,
condemning the innocent
so they can seize their wealth.
I hear the whispers among the women,
how they terrify young girls
into submitting to their lust.

I have seen them lurking in our garden
to spy on me. I send the gardeners
to work where they are hiding,
and watch from my window
as they sneak away.
Today I am safe.
I saw them leave with the others,
heading home
for their midday meal.

It is warm this noontime. I will bathe
in the coolness of our garden pool.
The maids have closed the gates.
I send them into the house
for oil and herbs.
How pleasant to be alone,
to remove my veil . . . .

What is that rustle in the bushes?

Nativity

There are no women here to help.
Joseph is midwife now.
In the bright starlight
through the stable doorway,
in the soft orange lamplight,
he kneels his sturdy bulk
at Mary's knees.
He has birthed calves and lambs.
His large, calloused hands
are gentle, sure.

The watching oxen jostle and snuffle
in their stalls,
their sweet breath steaming.

The angel's message has troubled him,
these long, waiting months,
but as the child slips, bloodied, crying,
into his hands,
baby arms outstretched,
he feels a rush of joy
binding him in love
to this divinity
whom he has given birth.

Judith and the Bridegroom

She is shadow within shadow, dust with the dust of millennia.

We cannot know her face or name. I see her as El Greco might have painted her: long dark hair, a pale, thin face, high cheekbones, a soft, warm mouth, her character showing in her great dark eyes. Her name? Perhaps her father, watching his newborn daughter fight for life, named her after one of the strong women in their tradition: Ruth, Esther, Deborah, Abigail, Judith. Let us call her Judith after the heroic woman, praised for her wisdom and beauty, who risked her life to save her people.

Girls in her tradition marry at thirteen or fourteen. Let us say she is a little older, perhaps fifteen. An only child, her mother ill since her birth. Her father does not want to let her go. He is the village scribe, and she is his companion, his helper, his son. Telling no one, he has taught her to read and write. She works with him, copying, writing letters and bills, documents of lesser importance. Not the Law, no—no woman can put her hand on that.

Let us say the Bridegroom is nineteen, late for marriage in his tradition. Men must marry young, be fruitful and multiply. He is the carpenter's son. The fathers have arranged the match. His family is not rich, but they have a reputation for honesty and for following the Law. Her father has watched the boy from childhood; he knows his wisdom, his gentleness, his scholarship in the Law. "Perhaps he will appreciate her," he thinks. "At least he will be kind."

The groom's mother looks at the bride's narrow hips. "Wait to start the babies," she warns her son. "Give her a chance to grow."

To his surprise and joy, the bridegroom finds a comrade in his bride, someone he can talk with as an equal. She tells him her secret, that she can read and write, and he, telling no one, teaches her the Law. They dispute together, arguing fine points of doctrine like two grandfathers in a corner. She sees in him the greatness that he doesn't yet see in himself, sees him groping in mind and soul toward a future hidden in gray mist.

They sing the song of songs together, and he rejoices when their child is on its way. Her joy has a somber edge, but she laughs as the baby dances in her womb whenever he is near. When her pains begin, she comes to him, carrying a small scroll wrapped with a red ribbon. "It is the song of songs," she says. "I made you a copy you can carry near your heart."

Then the women take her, lead her to the birthing room. The labor is long, agonizing. In her anguish, she calls his name, again and again. "I must be with her," he tells the women. "I must touch her," though he doesn't know how he knows. The women are scandalized. "The Law forbids it," and he lets them turn him away.

When it is over, they allow him to see her, still without touching her, following the Law. Washed and bound with the grave wrappings, the Spirit departed, she looks worn but accepting. The baby, his daughter, shrouded also in death, looks strong and bold, like the cherubim. Then their faces are covered, and they are gone from him.

After the funeral ceremonies, his face drawn, his eyes scalded by sleeplessness and grief, he comes to his mother. "I must go into the mountains, to be alone, to think. I believed I knew the Law, but now I have so many questions, so much I don't comprehend." His mother hands him his warm cloak and a bundle, bread and wine already prepared for him. "Go with our blessing."

Forty days later, he returns, thin, tired, dusty, but taller somehow, more wiry, and with a new glow of face and eyes. "I think it is time," his mother says. "When you have bathed and eaten, your father and I will tell you the story of your birth." He hears the tale with wonder. "And you both kept all this in your heart, all these years." He embraces them, weeping. "There is much to understand. Our cousin John has been preaching in the wilderness, a new teaching. I will join his disciples and study with them."

Rested, he sets out again, seeking his cousin. His mother watches him leave the village, sees him stop at the burial ground, stand before the tomb of Judith in prayer. Then he touches his hand to his breast and walks on.

*"Set me as a seal upon your heart, as a seal
upon your arm, for love is as strong as death."*

Panaya-Kapulu

The home, tradition says, of the Virgin Mary
on Nightingale Mountain, Ephesus

No pale blue, no pink and white,
for your images here.
In the shadowed alcove above your altar,
you are all dark bronze.
Moving slightly in the fluttering candle flames,
you smile gently at me,
inclining your head to my silent questions.
Your hands reach out in compassion.

At a side altar,
true Black Madonna,
you and your child gleam in your niche
in garments of gold and silver.
The matte ebony
of your faces, feet, hands,
absorbs all light.

Saint as Wise Woman,
in this shrine you manifest
Wisdom's dark dimension. Mystery.
Death and the life beyond.

Thomas, tradition says, was late again.
"She has died," the other apostles told him.
"She has gone. Passed on." Speaking
truer than they knew.
So he could say goodbye, they led him
where they had laid you. Lifting away the stone,
they saw your empty grave.
Your raising affirms the prophet's promise:
in my flesh I shall see God.

Mary of Egypt

Fifth Century C.E.   Feast Day: April 2

I sailed from Alexandria to the Holy Land,
paying my passage on my back.
I had been on the streets of Egypt since I was twelve.
Now I was on the streets of Jerusalem.
Cities are all the same to a whore.

The Blessed Virgin spoke to me:
"Cross over the Jordan."
For forty-seven years,
I have lived, a hermit in this desert.
A golden lion, my Lord Jesus, visits me,
teaches me scripture.
Once I sang the love songs of the streets.
Now I sing the love songs of the Psalms.

Last year a monk on pilgrimage
gave me communion.
He asked me,
"What do you miss most of your old life?"

I have pondered that question.
The food, I think.
I dream of the way
the Egyptians cook fish.
The herbs and the spices.
That's my temptation.
A table spread
with fragrant dishes.
I smell them in my sleep.
And I dream of the wines,
the red, the gold,
in jeweled goblets.
The wines...the wines...

Guadalupe / Tonantzin

In 1960, Our Lady of Guadalupe was named "Mother of the Americas" by Pope John XXIII. "Tonantzin" is the Aztec word for "Mother."

I knew how to handle the Spaniards.

With fire and axe they destroyed my temple here on Tepeyac Mountain. I wanted them to build me a new church, on this same spot, to recognize me and honor me as Mother of God.

"Devil!" they would have cried and burned my messenger, Juan Diego, at the stake, had I appeared to them in my Aztec image, the souvenir the tourists love. Tlazolteotl, crouching to give birth, grinning, grimacing with the effort, the head of the Son of God emerging between my thighs.

Cortez and his soldiers knew their own brown Virgin Mary, Guadalupe, Spanish patroness, Dark Madonna. I gave the Spaniards a demure young woman, brown skin, black hair, like their own dark virgin, like my own Aztec people. I told them my name was Tquatlasupe. Their ears heard Spanish, not Nahuatl, heard what they knew, Guadalupe.

"Show us a sign," the Bishop commanded Juan Diego when he brought my message. I gave them roses in winter and myself on his cloak, an image the scientists still can't analyze. Now, centuries later, hung above the basilica altar, I gleam undimmed in the colors of the quetzal, royal bird. The rising sun haloes my body. Stars trace constellations on my robe.

I am Mother of all, native and stranger, the weak and the mighty. I gather in my cloak the poor, the suffering, the homeless, as Juan Diego gathered my roses, my fragrant blossoms. Chavez raised my banner to rally the lettuce workers, the grape pickers. To those fighting tyranny, I am *Maria...Madre proletaria.*

My people were defeated, their gods smashed, but in me they see their victory. "Mother of the Americas." Tonantzin.

Praying the Labyrinth

Chartres Labyrinth
The Congregational Church, Exeter, N.H. , Dec. 31, 1999

I
Chemin de Jerusalem

Walking this labyrinth, I walk
the rocky, uneven streets of Jerusalem.
My eyes are on my shoes,
not on the holy places.
I use my cane for balance, place my feet
cautiously in the narrow, twisting way,
careful not to jostle the other pilgrims.
Not looking at them, I step aside
so they can pass. At the shrines,
I stay a moment only
so those crowded behind
can enter too. There is no time for prayer.

II
Labyrinth of Memory

On the last day of this era,
I walk four thousand years
into the past, into the womb of eternity,
center of pre-birth timelessness.
Hildegard's chants hallow the thin winter air.
I long to rest here, dream to the music,
but life pushes me out, birthing me.
My existence quartered by
this familiar path,
I exit where I came in,
into tomorrow.

III
On the Right Road

A pilgrim, returning from the center,
pauses at a labrys,
vertex of a hairpin curve.

"Which way do I go?"
"That way" Paralleling the way
he had traveled.
"But I just came from there."
"You won't walk the same road twice."

Exploring the path laid out for us
in its labyrinthine twists,
we appear to move, aimless,
away from our destination.
But, believing, we emerge,
surprising ourselves,
where we are supposed to be.

The eleven-circuit Chartres labyrinth   Robert Ferré
(www.labyrinthproject.com)

Seven Circuits: the Cretan Labyrinth

Kittery, Maine, autumn 2000

Climbing the hill, I glimpse among the trees
broken staubs of stone, standing
like stubs of shattered tombstones, carved slate
or marble, victim of storm or vandal, or
like native rocks on old New England gravesites,
placed to mark burials
when there was no money for carving.

On the hilltop the rocks reveal
their pattern. The foxfire path
spirals moonwise among trees, among stars.
I choose a white moonsnail shell for talisman,
follow the moon as it wanes to darkness.

In the surrounding mist,
pilgrims pace their millennial journey.
Generations of monks, encowled,
whisper their prayers.
Nuns in rough robes
counting their heavy wooden beads
walk their rosary circles
to join me at the labyrinth's hidden heart.

Returning with the waxing moon, I
place the shell in tribute on a stone
to mark my visit and emerge
from the buried past, waking
to the full moon's glory.

The seven-circuit Cretan labyrinth, courtesy of Loretta Rogers.
(www.angelfire.com/tn/SacredLabyrinth)

Dark Necessity

for R. J. H., Nov. 7

O my sister,
this is your cross,
citron and mauve,
mist rising from the spearpoint piercing its center.
You must pass alone with all your courage
through the black flower corpus,
spiraling down its throat into
the darkness at the heart of the earth.
There you wander blindly, twisting
through the labyrinth of the netherworld,
its rough, lichened walls your only guide.
Your feet stumble on the rocky path.
Voices cry out around you
in untranslatable moans.
The damp air smells of blood.

At the nadir of your journey waits
the giant malignant crab, stalked eyes glittering,
brandished claws gilded with phosphorescence.
The bubbles around his mouth
gleam in the dim light, oily rainbows.
You must fight him, this treacherous enemy,
elude his jagged pincers, to win
and return to the sunlight, leaving part of yourself
hanging on a meat hook, like Inanna.

Sister, do you remember?
When you were almost four, we went
for your first time, to visit at the beach.
All afternoon you played in the warm tide pools,
chasing the pink baby crabs,
peeking at the bigger ones, scarlet and cream,
dug backward into their sandy holes beneath the rocks,
claws tucked close, ready to snap
if little fingers came too near.

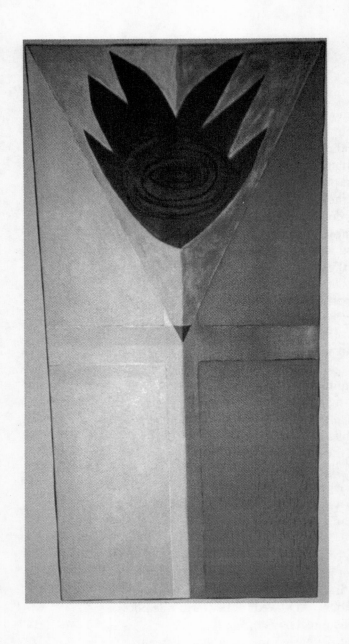

Black Flower   by Brigitte Keller: polymer/egg/wax emulsion

You ducked away as those great red claws struck out
when the big kids teased with sticks.

That evening, you walked in your sleep—
remember the story the aunts loved to tell?
You stood at the top of the stairs,
crying, "All the crabs, the crabs, the crabs."
Grownups rushed to you, reassuring,
held you, carried you back to bed,
stayed with you until the bad dreams were gone.

O sister,
now we gather to strengthen you in your bravery
as you ascend your cross.
Like Mother and the aunts, we will ease you
from your nightmare. Our care will succor you
like Grandfather Enki's little creatures,
who restored Inanna with their love.

The Poet as Lazarus

"Come out...come out."

My eyes open to blackness:
> What woke me?
> It is cool here. I am not in pain.
> There is cloth
> wrapped loosely around my head.
> Rough textured, clean smelling.
> I can breathe through it.
> The scent of herbs is strong but sweet.

> How long have I been here?
> Four days? Four years?
> Four lifetimes?
> I am not afraid.

> Is this a birth,
> wrapped like a newborn
> in swaddling clothes?
> It is very quiet here.

"Come out...."

> Shall I try to stand? Or do I
> want to lie still, go back
> to wherever I rested
> before I heard the whisper?

"Come out..."

One hand worked free,
I part the bindings covering my eyes.
Blackness.
Now the grating of a great rock moving:
       The sun is too strong for me.

"Lazarus, come forth."

       I know that voice.
       She is challenge.
       She is twelve hours of daylight.

       If I refuse,
       there will be no light in me.
       If I go walking by Her day,
       I will see the world bathed in light.

"If you believe, you will see
the glory of God."

As I rise, there is pain,
uncertainty. But Her voice
gives me courage.
I move, slowly, faltering,
shuffling with halting steps.
My hand, trailing its cerements,
supports me along the rough rock wall,
braces me in the sunlight
at the curving doorway.

"Unbind her. Let her go free."

More Readers' Comments:

Dance with Alpha and Omega—Jesus and Sheila-na-gig, Celtic guardian of doorways. Pat Parnell's humorous and healing portrayals of Medusa and Our Lady of Guadalupe, of Susanna and Sophia, touch chords in each of us. *Snake Woman* helps me laugh and pray about human possibility, divine grace, and our contemporary re-engagement with archetypal stories of the history of faith.
—MAREN TIRABASSI, Pastor, Northwood, N. H., Congregational Church of Christ. Author, *The Depth of Wells*; co-author, *Gifts of Many Cultures: Worship Resources for the Global Community* and *An Improbable Gift of Blessing: Prayers to Nurture the Spirit*. Poet Laureate, Portsmouth, NH, 2001

At the crossroads of this transitional era, it is again time for the healing wisdom of the Mother God, of holy women of history and mystery. Pat Parnell resurrects our cultural and Biblical sheroes: Miriam, Judith, Guadalupe, Mary, Susanna, Rizpah, Sophia. Through their love and their pain, Pat shows us possibilities for life, death, and rebirth. Our planet is crying out for this regenerative healing, for the rounding out of the image of God the Father to include the All-Loving Mother.
—PENELOPE MORROW, Women's Studies faculty, University of New Hampshire

About the Artists

BRIGITTE KELLER, York, Maine, has exhibited widely in this country and in Europe. She and Pat are partners in an artist/poet collaborative, "Sightings and Stanzas."

JESSICA E. KERN, Manchester, Vermont, is a graduate of White Pines College with a major in photography. *Humanity and Sin* appeared in *Compass Rose* with "Goddess: A Triptych."

KATE PARNELL is a student at Cooper Union. She accompanied Pat, her grandmother, on a pilgrimage to Greece and Turkey in the footsteps of St. Paul.

CHARLENE YELLE, Exeter, New Hampshire, is an artist and a jeweler.

About the Author

Pat Parnell with a tee-shirt from the National Museum, Dublin, Ireland, featuring the Celtic guardian spirit Sheila-na-gig.
(Photo by Tim Cook, Seacoast Newspapers)

Pat Parnell, Stratham, New Hampshire, a poet, teacher, and journalist, is Professor Emerita of Communications and Media at White Pines College, Chester, New Hampshire, where she is co-editor of *Compass Rose*, the White Pines journal of the literary and visual arts.

Her work appears in four recently-published anthologies, *HER WORDS*, edited by Burleigh Mutén; *Under the Legislature of Stars, 62 New Hampshire Poets; True Story*, by Rebecca Rule and Sue Wheeler; and *Anthology of New England Writers, 2001*.

A native of Richmond, Virginia, she taught on the secondary level in Fairfax County, Virginia, where she was adviser for the school literary magazine. For several years she taught advanced creative writing for the University of Virginia. She is part-owner and contributing editor of *The Journal* newspapers in King George, Virginia.

Pat and her husband Bill enjoy their extended family with its nucleus of four sons and ten grandchildren. Their mutual enthusiasms include reading, good food, Celtic music, politics, travel, and spiritual growth. Married since 1948, they now live in seacoast New Hampshire with their grey tiger cat, Nomar, and their Australian cattle dog, Sheila.

Readers' Comments, continued from back cover.

In her book, *Holy Personal,* Laura Chester describes a place "where creative expression joins hands with devotion." Pat Parnell has fashioned such a place: a shrine with many altars. These poems are images made of clay and wood and gemstone, set upon the altars amid guttering candles. Some are ancient and crudely wrought; some elegantly embellished; some evoke a smile (and the occasional burst of laughter); while others are dark, troubling. Parnell's images of the female—in all her manifestations—are crowded with the trappings of their times and locales, much the way altars become not only homages to the objects of devotion, but accretions, very personal histories of the journeys of the devotee. Poetic curator of this sacred place, Parnell is a fascinating guide.
—MARIE HARRIS, New Hampshire Poet Laureate. Author, *Weasel in the Turkey Pen* and *Your Sun, Manny*

Pat Parnell moves in an image-sensitive world where a few words on paper are enough to sketch complete scenes. She goes into the wilderness of long-forgotten gods and goddesses and brings them forward. Such an activity would have brought extreme danger in an intolerant, rigid society that took all imagery as being deadly serious...But what if the blending and inter-weaving of sacred stories were an art form as much appreciated as the rain which falls where it will? Then we'd all be waiting when she returned with her new-found friends! My favorite poem is "Apotheosis of Medusa," which brings Medusa into the sheltering presence of Mary, Queen of Heaven. Pat Parnell opens a path to unexpected enchantment and beauty.
—FR. BRIAN KENNEDY, C. S. s. R., Elko, Nevada.

(Excerpt from a letter, 9-18-00)
"Ariadne on Naxos" is a wonderful poem, and I am honored to have it dedicated to me. I wish you every blessing on your work.
—SUE MONK KIDD, author, *The Dance of the Dissident Daughter. A Woman's Journey from Christian Tradition to the Sacred Feminine.*

(More comments on p. 78)